Pitlochry Festival Theatre and Stellar Quines Present

SISTER RADIO

by Sara Shaarawi

Commissioned by Pearlfisher and Stellar Quines

First performed at Pitlochry Festival Theatre
on 25th August 2022

Cast and Creatives

Cast

Shirin	Nalân Burgess
Fatemeh	Lanna Joffrey

Creative Team

Writer / Director	Sara Shaarawi
Director	Caitlin Skinner
Set and Costume Designer	Becky Minto
Lighting Designer	Kate Bonney
Composer	Farzane Zamen
Movement Director	Saffy Setohy
Stage Manager	Kay Nicolson
Deputy Stage Manager (book)	Dayna Cumming
Assistant Stage Manager (book)	Alex Tosh

With special thanks to...

Maryam Hamidi, Neshla Caplan, Philip Howard, Henry Bell, Elizabeth Newman and Jemima Levick.

Cast

Lanna Joffrey – Fatemeh

Lanna Joffrey is an award-winning Iranian actor, spoken-word performer and writer working in the UK and US. She trained in acting at Royal Central School of Speech and Drama and Syracuse University. She has enjoyed performing extensively in theatre, film, audio projects and her spoken word, which has been published in print and online. Her critically acclaimed verbatim docudrama *Valiant* has toured throughout the UK/US and was published this year by NoPassport Press. She has been the narrator for Radio 4/BBC Book of the Week for *Maid* and *Worn*, the audiobook *An Emotion of Great Delight* and has recorded for numerous video games, commercials, audiodramas, animations and BBC Sounds/Darkfield Radio's *DEADHOUSE*. She also wrote/recorded for the podcast *Things I Am Not* (Legal Aliens Theatre).

Theatre credits include: *The Eyes of the Night* (Cervantes Theatre), *The Time of Our Lies* (Park Theatre), *Muse of Fire* and *Sonnet Walks* (Shakespeare's Globe), *A Thousand Splendid Suns* (A.C.T., Old Globe, Arena Stage and Seattle Rep), *Troilus and Cressida* and *Timon of Athens* (Willow Globe, The Factory), *I Call My Brothers* (Gate Theatre), *Soulless Ones* (Hammer House Live/Hoxton Hall), *They Promised Her the Moon* (Old Globe), *The Profane* (Playwrights Horizons), *Nine Parts of Desire* (Lyric Stage & The Kitchen), *Valiant* (Edinburgh Fringe, New York Fringe, WOW Festival, JW3, InterAct Theatre & Women & War Festival), *1001* (Denver Center). Film/TV credits include: *The First Circle*, *Druid Peak*, *Fishing Naked*, *Honk!*, *Security*, *Mad To Be Normal*, *Delocated* and *The New Americans*.

Awards include: NY Fringe (*Valiant*), IRNE (*Nine Parts of Desire*) and Ovation Award (*1001*).

Nalân Burgess – Shirin

Theatre credits include: *Welcome To Iran* (The National Theatre, & Theatre Royal Stratford East), *Out of Sorts* (Theatre503), *Where We Are: The Mosque* (The Arcola), *Citizen* (The Space Theatre), *My Beautiful Laundrette* (Above The Stag), *Nine the Musical* (Edinburgh Festival).

Television credits include: *The Sandman* (Warner Bros/DC Comics/Netflix), *Rude Boys* (BBC3).

Short plays include: *Who's Mom & Who's Mama?* (Theatre503), *Sexual Assault* (The Pleasance, London), *Rage Room* (Lyric Hammersmith), *A Tree Called Max* (The King's Head), *Horizon of the Irreversible Night* (The Arcola), *Dutty Wine* (The Bunker).

Film credits include: *Taarof*, *Meeting*, *House of Salem*, *Essex Boys: Retribution*, *He Who Dares.*

Radio and voice work includes: *Welcome To Iran* (BBC Radio), *An Undersea Story – Yakamoz/Bir Denizaltı Hikâyesi* (Netflix – dubbing), *The Offensive* (fiction podcast series), *Elite: Dangerous* (video game), *Jackie The Ripper* (fiction podcast series). *Boom* (fiction podcast series).

Sara Shaarawi – Writer

Sara Shaarawi is a playwright from Cairo based in Glasgow. She has had her work performed at the Tron Theatre (Glasgow), Lyceum Theatre (Edinburgh), Platform (Easterhouse), Rich Mix (London), Gate Theatre (London) and Tramway (Glasgow).

Sara also took part in the Playwrights' Studio Scotland's 2015 Mentoring Programme and the National Theatre of Scotland's Breakthrough Writers' programme in 2016.

In 2017 she was one of the recipients of the Playwrights' Studio Scotland's New Playwrights' Awards, and received a Starter programme bursary with the National Theatre of Scotland. Also in 2017, she partnered with the Workers Theatre to crowdfund and create Megaphone, a new bursary aimed at supporting artists of colour based in Scotland.

Other credits include performing in *One Day in Spring* (Oran Mor/NTS) and *Here's the News from Over There* (Northern Stage), and project managing the Arab Arts Focus showcase at the Edinburgh Fringe Festival 2017.

Caitlin Skinner – Director

Caitlin is Artistic Director and CEO of Stellar Quines Theatre Company. She is also one half of feminist theatre company Jordan & Skinner and director of new writing theatre company Pearlfisher. She is former Associate Director at Pitlochry Festival Theatre and former Artistic Director of the Village Pub Theatre.

Her recent directing credits include: *You've Never Slept in Mine* by Jenni Fagan (Stellar Quines/Edinburgh international Book Festival), *Hindu Times* by Jaimini Jethwa (Dundee Rep, Lyceum, EIF, Pitlochry Festival Theatre), *Distance Remaining* by Stewart Melton (Helen Milne Productions), *Alone* by Janey Godley (National Theatre of Scotland), *Five from Inside* by Rona Munro (Traverse Theatre), *Move* co-director (disaster plan), *Hope and Joy* (Pearlfisher/Stellar Quines), *A Brief History of the Fragile Male Ego*, *At A Stretch* and *Sanitise* (Jordan & Skinner), *Sunnyside Centre* (Village Pub Theatre), *Woke* (Apphia Campbell) and *The Strange Case of Jekyll and Hyde* (Lung Ha Theatre Company). She was also recently Associate Director on *Lament* for Sheku Bayoh by Hannah Lavery (National Theatre of Scotland).

Farzane Zamen – Composer

Farzane Zamen is an Iranian singer-songwriter and music producer based in Glasgow, Scotland. She has written and recorded in varied styles that include the Farsi songs of her homeland as well as progressive electronic music, shown off in her EP 'Z Bent'.

In 2017 she was awarded a prestigious Artist Protection Fund fellowship for artist residency hosted by CCA Glasgow. Before moving to Glasgow, Farzane worked as an underground musician in Iran, without having the opportunity to perform in public because of the Islamic laws applied in the country. After the revolution in 1979 women's solo voices were banned and many artists and singers had to leave the country.

After moving to Glasgow, Farzane has been very active in Glasgow's music scene and found herself more as a performing artist. She has taken part in important music festivals and events in Scotland and Europe, including Safe Havens (Malmö 2018), Celtic Connection (Glasgow 2019), Edinburgh Iranian Festival 2019, Solas Festival, etc.

She is a graduate of Glasgow School of Art with a degree in Master of Design Innovation and Service Design, and recently started working at Glasgow Women's Library as a Production Coordinator.

Saffy Setohy – Movement Director

Glasgow-based Saffy Setohy is a dance artist working across choreography, performance, participatory work, facilitation, mentoring and movement direction in an expanded field. Trained in London at Trinity Laban, interdisciplinary collaboration is at the heart of her work. She has made various collaborative works for different contexts, presented across the UK and internationally.

Movement direction credits for theatre include: *Niqabi Ninja*, written by Sara Shaarawi and directed by Amanda Gough, *The Bridge,* written and directed by Annie George, *Twa*, written by Annie Geroge and directed by Saffy, *REd*, devised and directed by Tidy Carnage Theatre/Allie Butler.

Saffy's choreographic projects have been commissioned by organisations including Tramway, Science Gallery London, UZ Arts, The Touring Network, Southeast Dance, CCN Le Havre, Dansefestival Barents. She has been an associate artist of Insitu

European network for art in public space, an emerging artist in residence at the Southbank Centre (2010–2012), and recipient of the Saltire Society/Scottish Dance Theatre Choreographer bursary. Saffy is currently Glasgow Life Artist in Residence for Canal Ward in the North of the city, facilitating a community-led arts and ecology project creatively occupying 'derelict and vacant' land. Saffy enjoys supporting other artists and is currently mentoring dance artist Julia McGhee in developing *The Morrich Project*. This responds to Julia's relationship with her home in the Scottish Highlands, a coastal ecology of special scientific interest, and a live air weapons range. Saffy is currently Co-Chair and artist member of The Work Room, an artist-led organisation supporting the development of choreographic practice.

Becky Minto – Set and Costume Designer
Becky has been designing for over 25 years for companies including National Theatre Scotland, Upswing Aerial Theatre Company, Fire Exit, Royal Lyceum, All Or Nothing Aerial Dance Company, Grid Iron, Perth Rep, Visible Fictions, Vanishing Point, Scottish Dance Theatre, Lung Ha, 7:84, The Byre, The Citizen's Theatre, Walk The Plank and Dundee Rep. Designs for Pitlochry Festival Theatre are *Hard Times, Europe, Para Handy* and *The Rise and Fall of Little Voice.* Her work covers main house productions, large-scale touring, aerial and circus indoor and outdoor productions, multiple site-specific designs and large outdoor ceremonies, including the as Associate Designer for the Opening Ceremony and Designer for the Closing Ceremony for Glasgow 2014 Commonwealth Games.

She was awarded the Silver medal for Space Design for *The 306: Dawn* for the National Theatre of Scotland at the World Stage Design exhibition in Taipei 2017. Her designs have been selected as part of the UK exhibition for The British Society of Theatre Designers at the Prague Quadrennial PQ19, PQ15, PQ11 and PQ07.

Future productions include: *Lena* (Feather Productions), *The Wonderful Story of Henry Sugar* (Perth Theatre, Helen Milne Productions and The Roald Dahl Story Company), *Spike* (Starcatchers), *Helping Hands*, *Sister Radio* (Pitlochry Festival Theatre), *Underwood Lane* co-design with John Byrne (Tron Theatre), *Wilf* (Traverse Theatre) and *Ghost Hunter* (Visible Fictions).

Kate Bonney – Lighting Designer

Kate first worked with Pitlochry Festival Theatre back in 2003, a few months after graduating from the Royal Scottish Academy of Music and Drama, so is delighted to be working on the 2022 season, marking twenty years of association with the company which has remained close to her heart throughout. She recently worked on *Christmas Tales* with the Lyceum, Edinburgh; *Oh Yes We Are!* with Perth Theatre; *Barefoot in the Park* with Pitlochry Festival Theatre and the Lyceum; *The Cheviot, The Stag and the Black, Black Oil* with Dundee Rep and The National Theatre of Scotland; *Ulster American* with the Traverse Theatre, Edinburgh; *Bingo! The Musical* with Grid Iron and Stellar Quines; *Passing Places* with Dundee Rep; *306: Day* with National Theatre of Scotland and *Red Shed* with Mark Thomas, as well as designing for such other companies as: Scottish Opera, Tron Theatre, Scottish Youth Theatre, Pitlochry Festival Theatre, Birds of Paradise and Lyric Theatre Belfast. Kate has also led the design for the award-winning Enchanted Forest in Highland Perthshire since 2013 and is Creative Director of event design company Lightworks.

PITLOCHRY FESTIVAL THEATRE

For over seventy years, we've been Highland Perthshire's artistic heart and soul, sitting perched on the edge of the River Tummel and looking out to Ben-y-Vrackie, the spectacular 'Speckled Mountain'.

Now attracting over 100,000 visitors each year, we're not just a venue. We're famous for producing large-scale plays and musicals that delight theatregoers of all ages. International-standard performances featuring award-winning artists, writers and directors, and outstanding set and costume designs all combine to bring audiences to their feet.

Stellar
•ᴼQuines

Stellar Quines is an intersectional feminist theatre company based in Scotland. We believe theatre is a force for change, for collaborating with others and building inclusive coalitions.

We create shows, provide opportunities and support for career development, both on stage and backstage, for creatives at all levels. We commission research and join forces with others to campaign for change. We take our work out into the community with projects that nurture creativity and invite action, all with the aim of achieving greater equality.

www.stellarquines.co.uk

PEARLFISHER
NEW PLAYS FOR SCOTLAND

Pearlfisher is a new theatre company which commissions and develops new plays for production in Scotland and beyond. Allied to this is a fresh approach to talent development, working with emerging artists in all areas of performance and production, and cultivating paid apprenticeships and assistantships.

Sara Shaarawi

Sister Radio

Salamander Street

PLAYS

Published in 2022 by Salamander Street Ltd,
272 Bath Street, Glasgow, G2 4JR (info@salamanderstreet.com).

PB ISBN: 9781914228834

10 9 8 7 6 5 4 3 2 1

Further copies of this publication can be purchased from
www.salamanderstreet.com

NOTES ON THE TEXT:

- The play takes place over two timelines simultaneously. The scenes that take place in the past should not feel like flashbacks, they should feel more like echoes, ripples, hauntings. The effect is one of double exposure in photography, where one timeline is layered on to another. Throughout the play one should feel like the past and the present are living together.

- The same double exposure effect extends to the physical space. The setting is always the living room/kitchen of their Edinburgh flat, but it's not a static space, it's a space that holds the characters' entire life experience. It is both Edinburgh and Tehran, it is the '70s and the now.

- One of the (many) shared rituals the sisters have is reading coffee grains. It's bad luck to read your own grains (and your own fortune) which is why they do this. In the 2020 timeline they always do this in silence, but I have offered interpretations of what they're reading in the stage directions. This is not just an offering to the actors but to the entire creative team to interpret them (or not) as they wish.

- The silent scenes set in 2020 should be used as guides rather as prescription. The domestic tasks and shared rituals can be adapted by the company, as long as it doesn't significantly shift the narrative (i.e reading the coffee grains).

Scene One

An Edinburgh flat.

The room is well-lived in, elegantly decorated and very cosy.

The kitchen is well stocked and slightly too small for the amount of kitchenware and tableware it has, that's because it's also piled high with various types of tea, spices, condiments and snacks.

A radio switches on. Static. Then the voices of two children come through.

RADIO: Good morning ladies and gentlemen!

Giggles in the background.

RADIO: I would like to welcome you all to our show. My name is Fatemeh and I am your host this evening. This is my sister, Shirin.

Hello.

And this is… Sister Radio!

Sounds of a children-made theme tune.

RADIO: This is a show where we talk about everything… Umm… Today we are exploring our garden with our special guest… Uhhh… Dr. Azi – no, um… Dr. Shapour!

One child applause and more giggling.

RADIO: Welcome doctor. So… What can you tell me about this garden?

Well… This garden is very special. There's lots to explore, I like to wait for the lemons to grow so I pick them, and I like to catch the crickets, like this… See? One other thing I like to do is lift these big rocks here. Because see…?

Screams followed by hysterical laughter.

RADIO: Fatemeh! Where are you going? It's just beetles! They're more scared of us than we are of them!

The radio starts to fade out and music starts to fade in, filling the space. It hasn't decided where in time it is yet.

It's 2020. An older **SHIRIN** *enters the kitchen and makes herself a cup of tea.*

It's also 1978. A younger **FATEMEH** *walks in. She starts to decorate the house.*

SHIRIN *watches the memory of her sister as she does this.*

FATEMEH *switches the radio to Iranian pop music and starts to dance.*

SHIRIN *joins* **FATEMEH** *in a few steps, takes her cup of tea and goes back into her room. She takes the present time with her.*

We are now fully in the '70s.

Suddenly a younger **SHIRIN** *bursts in, carrying a particularly ornate samovar.*

SHIRIN: Look what I found!

FATEMEH: Where did you get that?

SHIRIN: That shop down the road.

FATEMEH: What shop down the road?

SHIRIN: The one that sells junk.

FATEMEH: What are you talking about?

SHIRIN: The one that sells dead people's things!

FATEMEH: The antique shop?

SHIRIN: Is that what they call it here?

FATEMEH: The shop that sells antiques. The antique shop, yes.

SHIRIN: What a scam.

FATEMEH: What are we going to do with a samovar?

SHIRIN: Make tea, obviously.

FATEMEH: We never learned to make tea.

SHIRIN: YOU never learned to make tea.

FATEMEH: And you did?

SHIRIN: I did. I learned how to make PROPER tea.

FATEMEH: Make us some proper tea then.

SHIRIN: I will.

FATEMEH: Come on.

SHIRIN: We need the right type of tea.

FATEMEH: Right.

SHIRIN: Yes.

FATEMEH: Let's get the right tea then.

SHIRIN: What, now?

FATEMEH: Yes.

SHIRIN: But I just came from outside!

FATEMEH: So?

SHIRIN: It's freezing out there!

FATEMEH: It's always freezing.

Come on.

SHIRIN: But I'm tired!

FATEMEH: You're not getting out of this, little sister. You're going to prove to me that you can make tea with a samovar.

SHIRIN: You're so annoying…

FATEMEH: Let's go. I also don't have any coal.

SHIRIN: Coal? Why do we need coal?

The memory fades and it's 2020.

The samovar now sits in the living room as decor. It hasn't been used in years.

FATEMEH *stands at the doorway, watching their younger selves leave the flat.*

She switches the radio to another station. She starts to make tea.

SHIRIN *comes out of her room and begins to assemble biscuits and sandwiches.*

Date and Rose Water.

Cheddar and Piccalilli.

Smoked Salmon and Cream Cheese.

Orange and Cardamom.

Roast Beef and Horseradish.

Chickpea and Pistachio.

FATEMEH *fusses over presentation.*

SHIRIN *smokes out the window.*

A phone rings.

SHIRIN: Hello?

It's Maryam, their niece.

SHIRIN: Hello darling, we're just waiting for you, the tea's almost ready.

Oh no. What's happened? How come? Does she have a fever?

Poor thing. Yes, of course we're more than happy to postpone!

Lots of hot fluids. I can drop off some chicken soup tomorrow.

Nonsense! Of course it's no trouble! I made a promise to your mother, you don't want us disturbing her in death now, I will make Nahid some chicken soup. Her grandmother's recipe, so her spirit is there with her.

Yes, she's here, would you like to talk to her? Of course darling, one moment.

She hands the phone to **FATEMEH**.

FATEMEH: Hello azizam, what's wrong? What's all this talk of fever?

Oh no! Have you taken her to hospital? No? Well, you know me, I worry about these things.

Make her some quince tea. Do you know how? Good. I'm glad your mother passed on the family secret. Do you need me to get you some quince seeds? I'm happy to pick some up.

Alright. Alright darling, no problem.

Nonsense, you've given us a treat, your aunties are going to have a feast now!

Maybe we can do something for Nowruz? Perfect. I will call you to organise and send my love to the little ones.

Alright darling, thank you, take care of yourself. Goodbye.

Silence.

This is disappointing.

At least there's biscuits.

They each eat a sandwich.

SHIRIN *has a cup of tea, no milk with two sugars, and a couple of biscuits.*

FATEMEH *doesn't.*

Time to clear the mess.

FATEMEH *puts the empty cups and plates in the kitchen.*

SHIRIN *washes them up.*

They work together.

They never make eye contact.

It doesn't feel uncomfortable.

It feels…harmonious.

SHIRIN *puts away all the leftovers.*

FATEMEH *starts to make Turkish coffee.*

SHIRIN *sits down to read her book.*

FATEMEH *pours the coffee into two small cups with saucers.*

She brings over the coffee and turns the TV on.

This annoys **SHIRIN** *but she doesn't say anything.*

They both drink their coffee.

When the finish their coffee, they move their cups in a rotating motion, put the saucer on the cup and flip it.

They put the saucers back on the table.

They wait for the cups to cool down.

SHIRIN *reads.*

FATEMEH *watches TV. She reacts to a plot twist.*

They don't speak.

They don't make eye contact.

It doesn't feel uncomfortable.

FATEMEH *takes her sister's cup and reads the coffee grains.*

SHIRIN *takes her sister's cup and reads the coffee grains.*

They do this in silence.

There's chatter and noise followed by sudden silence.

Thick patterns of grains, this is worry hanging in the air.

A fish! Money will be coming in or leaving your house.

Papers, lots of papers, you'll have a lot of news.

There's a small heart. Someone cares for you.

There's a horse, that's a very good omen. Progress.

They finish their reading.

SHIRIN *smokes her last cigarette of the day.*

FATEMEH *puts on the radio and washes the cups.*

FATEMEH *goes to the bathroom to brush her teeth, then she goes into her room and closes the door.*

She doesn't say goodnight.

SHIRIN *finishes her cigarette.*

She tries to close the window. She struggles.

She remembers the technique. She tries it and finally the window shuts.

She finishes tidying the kitchen.

She eats one last biscuit.

Soft hysterical laughter comes from the radio.

She turns off the radio and the lights.

She also goes to bed.

Scene Two

August 1978.

The flat is empty, we can hear the sounds of two people lugging some very heavy luggage up three flights of stairs.

Finally, the door opens, and the women burst in.

FATEMEH: Oh god. What do you have packed in there? Bricks?

SHIRIN: It's just books.

FATEMEH: Did you really need to bring all of your books?

SHIRIN: Yes.

FATEMEH: We have books in this country as well you know.

SHIRIN: Not in Farsi.

FATEMEH: True. I can recite them to you in Farsi.

SHIRIN: Your Farsi's shit these days.

FATEMEH: How dare you?

SHIRIN: I speak the truth.

FATEMEH: I was going to offer you some tea but now you've got to make your own.

SHIRIN: I'll make the tea for both of us.

FATEMEH: I was joking!

SHIRIN: I'm not, I'm your guest, it's the least I can do.

FATEMEH: You're not a guest. This is your home now.

SHIRIN: Not yet. I just arrived, it's not my space yet. Not my home.

FATEMEH: Is that so?

FATEMEH *lights a cigarette.*

SHIRIN: Fatemeh! How could you!

FATEMEH: What?

SHIRIN: What do you mean what? The smoking!

FATEMEH: I just… I like it.

SHIRIN: You like it? How long have you been a smoker?

FATEMEH: Not long.

SHIRIN: How long?

FATEMEH: A year. Maybe two, something like that.

SHIRIN: Two years!

FATEMEH: I'm not a proper smoker, I just… like it sometimes.

SHIRIN: It's disgusting.

FATEMEH: Did you ever try it?

SHIRIN: No.

FATEMEH: Come on, have a go.

SHIRIN: No never!

FATEMEH: Come on Shishi, share a cigarette with your sister.

SHIRIN *gives in, not to make her sister happy, just out of curiosity. She takes a puff, coughs and immediately gives it back.*

SHIRIN: It burns! Arrgghh, that's horrible!

FATEMEH: You get used to it.

SHIRIN: Keep that stuff away from me. Oh god how disgusting.

FATEMEH: Stop being such a baby!

SHIRIN: Stop smoking!

FATEMEH: How do you take your tea?

SHIRIN: Just sugar.

FATEMEH: You haven't converted to milk yet?

SHIRIN: The British have destroyed the pleasure of drinking tea.

FATEMEH: Don't hold back.

SHIRIN: At least open a window or something, I don't want to die of suffocation.

FATEMEH: When did you become so melodramatic?

SHIRIN *tries to open the window. She struggles.* **FATEMEH** *helps her and together they manage to get it open.*

SHIRIN: Why are the windows so hard to open here!

FATEMEH: It's cold.

SHIRIN: How can you live like this?

FATEMEH: It's not that bad. It's a beautiful city.

SHIRIN: Why didn't you go somewhere with a bit more character? Like London.

FATEMEH: Stop being such a grouch.

SHIRIN: Or somewhere exciting? Like America.

FATEMEH: America is violent.

SHIRIN: Everywhere is violent!

FATEMEH: I like Edinburgh.

SHIRIN: Why did Baba insist we come here? Why send your children to Britain of all places!

FATEMEH: Shirin…

SHIRIN: Just because he got his education here doesn't mean we should as well.

I don't know if I'll ever forgive him.

FATEMEH: Of course you'll forgive him. He's our father. At least you weren't sent to boarding school like Paria.

We should remember to call her later.

SHIRIN: I hate this.

FATEMEH: Hate what?

SHIRIN: Familial obligation. Why should I owe him anything for creating me? I didn't ask to be created, and not by him.

FATEMEH: How do you know you didn't ask to be created?

SHIRIN: What do you mean?

FATEMEH: Do you never get the urge?

SHIRIN: What urge?

FATEMEH: The urge to have babies, a family.

SHIRIN: No. I've never had 'the urge.'

FATEMEH: Really?

SHIRIN: Really. Why? Do you get the urge?

FATEMEH: Sometimes. Yes.

SHIRIN: Okay.

FATEMEH: And I guess… I wonder if that's maybe the call for creation. Maybe you did ask for it, maybe we all did.

SHIRIN: What…on earth are you talking about?

FATEMEH: It was just a thought.

SHIRIN: Are you sure you're alright? What are the Scots feeding you?

FATEMEH: Shut up!

SHIRIN: Call for creation, where did that come from?

FATEMEH: It sounded better in my head.

SHIRIN: Well it should have stayed in your head!

FATEMEH: Right you're getting milk in your tea.

SHIRIN: No, no Fatemeh I'm sorry, no!

Don't do this to me! I'm your sister!

The memory fades.

Scene Three

March 2020.

SHIRIN *walks into the room. She's in a dressing gown, a winter coat and a hat.*

SHIRIN *makes her morning coffee, black, no sugar.*

SHIRIN *makes her sister's coffee, black with sugar. She leaves it in the kitchen.*

SHIRIN *makes herself some breakfast.*

FATEMEH *walks into the room. She's dressed.*

She notices the open window and realises why it's so cold.

She tries to close it. No luck.

Great.

She looks for her tools, they're out of WD-40, she looks for the grocery list and adds it on.

She goes into her room to layer up.

SHIRIN *turns on the radio.*

It's the ten o'clock news.

It's about the virus in China.

There's a couple of cases in the UK.

Nothing to worry about.

Many cases in Italy.

But things are okay here.

Supermarkets try to prevent stockpiling.

Because everything is fine here.

Harry and Meghan leave Royals.

UK has plans to deal with the pandemic.

Brexit.

Family abductions in Dubai.

Priti Patel is a bully.

FATEMEH *emerges dressed in several layers. She sits down to have her coffee.*

SHIRIN *switches the radio to some music. It's one of those pop songs about existential dread.*

She washes her dishes.

FATEMEH *makes herself some breakfast.*

SHIRIN *goes to the bathroom to shower.*

FATEMEH *dances a bit despite herself.*

Then she hears her sister's voice coming from the radio.

RADIO: 'Forgive her.
  Sometimes she forgets
  she is painfully the same
  as stagnant water,
  hollow ditches,
  foolishly imagines
  she has the right to exist.'

  It's Forough. She's incredible. Isn't she, Fatemeh?

The radio continues playing the pop song

FATEMEH *remembers something and adds it to the grocery list.*

SHIRIN *is now dressed.*

She puts on her shoes. They're bright and colourful.

She remembers herself at eighteen.

She would never have worn such shoes.

Or coloured her hair.

She wishes she had worn her hair short.

She wishes she had been more adventurous.

She grabs the list from the kitchen.

FATEMEH *remembers she needs something else but it's too late now.*

The list is gone.

SHIRIN *grabs a tote bag.*

She heads out. But not before hiding the TV remote.

FATEMEH *tries to switch off the radio, but the voices keep pouring through.*

This isn't unusual.

RADIO: Welcome! Welcome to our radio show…

    Isn't she incredible?

    When we go back to Tehran…

    I'M YOUR SISTER!

FATEMEH *looks for the TV remote. She can't find it. The echoes continue.*

RADIO: Stop Fatemeh. Stop it!

    Tell me.

    You're not my mother.

    Is it love?

    Your Farsi is shit these days.

    I'm sorry. I'm sorry. I'm sorry.

FATEMEH *realises what her sister has done, grabs the cigarettes and hides them.*

RADIO: There are still demonstrations.

A revolution, Fatemeh!

Please.

I'm scared.

Is it love?

What do you want from me?

Answer me.

FATEMEH: Enough!

The flat is now silent again.

And **FATEMEH** *sits with her memories.*

Scene Four

September 1978. The radio is on. News snippets.

25,000 die in 7.7 earthquake in Iran.

US performs nuclear tests.

Ayatollah Khomeini calls for an uprising in the Iranian Army.

USSR performs nuclear tests.

Anwar Sadat, Jimmy Carter and Menachem Begin sign Camp David Accords.

The radio fades into soft music.

SHIRIN *is sitting on the couch reading a book of poetry by Forough Farrokhzad, she's totally engrossed and keeps taking a moment to process the words.* **FATEMEH** *is studying at the kitchen table, she watches her sister curiously. They are both dressed in a ridiculous amount of layers. They each have an overturned coffee cup beside them.*

FATEMEH: What are you reading?

SHIRIN: *(startled)* Fatemeh! you scared me. I forgot you were there.

FATEMEH: Is it that good?

SHIRIN: This book? It's brilliant, Fatemeh. Forough Farrokhzad's poetry.

FATEMEH: Ah.

SHIRIN: Listen to this:

'In that dark and silent private place
I sat, distracted, by his side
His lips poured passion upon mine
I was saved from my mad heart's sorrows'

FATEMEH: Hmm…

SHIRIN: What do you mean 'hmm'?

FATEMEH: I mean, as beautiful as that is, she was still a whore.

SHIRIN: FATEMEH!

FATEMEH: She left her son. What kind of woman does that?

SHIRIN: I don't think it's a simple as that. They took him away from her.

FATEMEH: Because she couldn't keep her legs crossed.

SHIRIN: Men have affairs all the time, why can't women?

FATEMEH: I'm not saying she can't have affairs. I'm just saying she knew what would happen if she did, and she did it anyway. I'm just saying it as it is.

SHIRIN: Her poetry is incredible. I want to write poetry like hers.

FATEMEH: Because the world needs more poetry?

SHIRIN: Yes actually. I think the world needs more poetry. From women.

FATEMEH: Maybe.

SHIRIN: I want to know what that feels like.

FATEMEH: Writing poetry?

SHIRIN: No. Passion. Desire. Love.

What do you think it's like?

FATEMEH: …

SHIRIN: Fatemeh?

FATEMEH: …what?

SHIRIN: Are you…?

FATEMEH: Am I what?

SHIRIN: Oh my god. Are you in a…relation?

FATEMEH: Relation?

SHIRIN: Like a love relation? Passion?

Oh god… Fatemeh… Have you had sex?

FATEMEH: …

I've had a man in my life lately. Yes.

SHIRIN: *(gasps)*

FATEMEH: It's not a big deal.

SHIRIN: It's a huge deal! Why didn't you tell me?

FATEMEH: You wanted me to write it in my letters? You think I trust
Baba to not read them?

SHIRIN: Who is he?

FATEMEH: He's just someone I met.

SHIRIN: How did you meet?

FATEMEH: He's a friend of a friend.

SHIRIN: But where did you actually meet?

FATEMEH: Well, the first time we actually met was at a concert.

SHIRIN: You went to a concert?

FATEMEH: Yes.

SHIRIN: Who are you?

FATEMEH: I have my life here.

SHIRIN: So you met at a concert and fell in love?

FATEMEH: No.

FATEMEH *gets up and picks up her sister's coffee cup. She begins to examine it. The conversation is a bit much for her, but she's also really enjoying it.*

SHIRIN: No?

FATEMEH: We didn't really talk then.

SHIRIN: What kind of love story is this?

FATEMEH: We met at a concert, and at the time the bathtub was broken so he offered to come fix it.

SHIRIN: You asked a strange man to fix your bathtub!

FATEMEH: I didn't ask him, he offered. And he wasn't a stranger, he was a friend of a friend.

SHIRIN: So you're dating a handyman?

FATEMEH: No. He works at a warehouse.

SHIRIN: Can you ask him to fix our window?

FATEMEH: What? No.

SHIRIN: Why not!

FATEMEH: Why don't you fix it? You broke it.

SHIRIN: I opened it. That's what windows do.

FATEMEH: Well look here.

FATEMEH *indicates the cup in her hand.*

FATEMEH: See this? Lots of noise. You should be careful of gossip.

SHIRIN: Shut up. This isn't gossip, this is the impossible. Ms. Perfect has turned into Baba's worst nightmare. I mean, nothing I do will ever surpass this!

FATEMEH: You can't tell him!

SHIRIN: Are you joking? Of course I won't tell him.

FATEMEH: There's also a cross here. A little one. There might be some loss or trouble.

SHIRIN: What's his name?

FATEMEH: John.

SHIRIN: John.

FATEMEH: Yes, John.

SHIRIN: British!

FATEMEH: Yes.

SHIRIN: The enemy!

FATEMEH: He's Scottish. If you want to get technical.

SHIRIN: You're fraternising with the enemy!

FATEMEH: Fraternising?

SHIRIN: How long?

FATEMEH: How long what?

SHIRIN: How long have you been with…with…John?

FATEMEH: A year.

SHIRIN: A YEAR!

FATEMEH: Yes.

SHIRIN: I need to sit down.

   I don't think my heart can take this.

FATEMEH: You have an old figure here, see the profile? A mentor maybe?

SHIRIN: I can't believe this. You're in love?

FATEMEH: There's a new moon. The start of a new phase maybe?

SHIRIN: Fatemeh answer!

FATEMEH: Yes.

SHIRIN: Yes you're in love?

FATEMEH: I think so, yes. I think.

SHIRIN: What's it like?

FATEMEH: There's a snake here as well, all curled up. Careful with who you trust.

SHIRIN: Tell me!

FATEMEH: Okay…

I feel…really nervous when I'm around him. I don't know why, but I'm always excited to see him and scared…scared of knowing what I want and not knowing what he wants.

SHIRIN: Wow.

FATEMEH: When he smiles at me, I feel like…I've won at a game that I didn't even know I was playing. When I'm around him I'm always hoping he'll make eye contact or put his arm around me or touch me in some way and then when he does do that it's like…we're speaking a private language, exchanging secrets, sharing thoughts but without speaking. And sometimes when I'm with him…I feel like I'm escaping into another world, just for a little while, a world where no one knows me and I can just be me, without all the…expectations. It's like time stops, and it's just the two of us and that's it.

SHIRIN: Wow.

FATEMEH: Just wow?

SHIRIN: I mean…that sounds amazing.

FATEMEH: It is…it's really nice.

SHIRIN: Will I meet him?

FATEMEH: Do you want to?

SHIRIN: Of course!

FATEMEH: I'll invite him for dinner then.

SHIRIN: Dinner here?

FATEMEH: Yes, why not?

SHIRIN: He eats your cooking?

FATEMEH: Watch it, Shishi.

SHIRIN: And he's still alive and well?

FATEMEH: How dare you?

SHIRIN: Are you sure he's human?

FATEMEH: *(laughing)* Stop!

The memory fades.

Scene Five

March 2020.

SHIRIN *comes back in with the groceries. She keeps her coat on, turns on the radio, turns to the classical music channel and starts to put away the groceries.*

She puts a box of fresh scones down in front of **FATEMEH** *along with a newspaper.*

SHIRIN *makes tea for the both of them.*

She sits across from **FATEMEH** *with her own newspaper.*

They silently have tea and scones.

FATEMEH *does the crossword.*

SHIRIN *starts looking for her cigarettes.*

She can't find them.

She looks at her sister intently.

FATEMEH *ignores her knowingly.*

SHIRIN *gives up.*

FATEMEH *gets up, grabs a tote bag and goes out.*

SHIRIN *brings out the remote from its hiding place.*

She goes into the kitchen and moves her sister's favourite mug into a different cupboard.

Voices start to filter through the music.

RADIO: Welcome to another episode of SISTER RADIO! Today's extra special guest is the poet… Forough Farrokhzad!

A young woman recites a poem.

RADIO: 'I have sinned, a delectable sin
   In an embrace which was ardent, like fire
   I have sinned in the midst of arms
   Which were hot and vengeful, like iron'

The radio tunes out…

Scene Six

November 1978.

The radio is on.

Snippets of news.

Sid Vicious charged with murder of girlfriend Nancy Spungen.

Pope John Paul II is elected.

Dominica gains independence from Great Britain.

Iranian troops fire on anti-Shah student protesters by Tehran University.

900 members of The People's Temple take their own lives and that of their children under the leadership of Jim Jones.

It looks like there was a little get-together, **SHIRIN** *and* **FATEMEH** *are clearing up plates, cups and bottles of beer.*

They do this in silence.

FATEMEH: …

SHIRIN: …

Still not saying anything.

FATEMEH: Say something!

SHIRIN: Don't scare me like that!

FATEMEH: So?

SHIRIN: What?

FATEMEH: Aren't you going to say anything?

SHIRIN: What do you want me to say?

FATEMEH: You hated him.

SHIRIN: I didn't say anything!

FATEMEH: Exactly! You always have something to say.

SHIRIN: Fatemeh...

FATEMEH: He's not always so awkward, you know.

SHIRIN: I didn't think he was awkward.

FATEMEH: You could have been nicer.

SHIRIN: I was nice!

FATEMEH: He was trying really hard you know, you could have at least
tried to –

SHIRIN: I don't understand what I did!

FATEMEH: You always ruin everything!

SHIRIN: What did I ruin?

FATEMEH: I don't care what you think. I don't care if you don't like him.
It doesn't change anything.

SHIRIN: Fatemeh can you hear yourself?

FATEMEH: ...

I just wanted you to like him.

SHIRIN: I do. I do like him.

FATEMEH: You're just saying that.

SHIRIN: No really. He seems nice.

FATEMEH: Just nice?

SHIRIN: Fatemeh we've only met once. I think he's alright. He's very…
Scottish.

FATEMEH: What's wrong with Scottish?

SHIRIN: Nothing. It's just…a bit strange.

FATEMEH: What do you mean?

SHIRIN: It's quite a commitment.

FATEMEH: To him?

SHIRIN: To your life here.

Or are you thinking of taking him to Tehran?

FATEMEH: I don't know… I haven't thought that far ahead…

I can't imagine him in Iran.

SHIRIN: Can you imagine yourself here?

FATEMEH: You mean forever?

SHIRIN: Can you imagine yourself old here?

FATEMEH: Why not?

SHIRIN: It's just a strange thought.

FATEMEH: …

SHIRIN: I can't imagine being old anywhere but Tehran.

FATEMEH: I don't think about getting old.

SHIRIN: When I picture myself old, it's in our house with Baba's old
carpets and Mama's library. It'll be probably just me and Forough. It's
all I need, her words.

FATEMEH: …

SHIRIN: We won't be distracted by silly men.

FATEMEH: Unbelievable.

SHIRIN: What?

FATEMEH: You're so patronising sometimes.

SHIRIN: I was just imagining what it would be like –

FATEMEH: Distracted by silly men? Is that what you think of me?

SHIRIN: What? No Fatemeh, I didn't mean it like that!

FATEMEH: You said it.

SHIRIN: Fatemeh you're being completely absurd!

FATEMEH: And you're being a total...cunt!

FATEMEH *storms out of the room, clearly upset, slamming the door behind her.*

SHIRIN: Love has clearly rotted your brain!

The memory fades...

Scene Seven

April 2020.

FATEMEH *is making coffee.*

The TV is on, they're watching the news.

It's a global pandemic.

People are dying.

The world is locked down.

It's scary.

SHIRIN's *cell phone rings.*

SHIRIN: Hello darling.

Yes, we've been watching the news.

I know. I know, it's hard to tell what he means.

We're alright for now. I managed to do a big shop before the shops emptied out.

Don't worry azizam. I also go to the Asian shops and they were still pretty full when I went so we're well stocked for the next wee while.

Thank you darling. Thank you.

Yes, I think it's best to stay in for now.

Don't worry, you have a family to take care of. Yes of course we're family too, but you have little ones to look after.

Yes, they called for your aunt but she declined, you know because of my…health and such.

Of course. What would I do without her? She takes very good care of me.

No, no, no, there's absolutely no need.

We're going to have our coffee now and we're fine. I promise.

Of course, of course I'll let you know if we need anything.

Alright darling. Okay, keep in touch, send my love to all.

Okay, bye lovely.

FATEMEH *brings the coffee over.*

They drink.

FATEMEH *is uncomfortable.*

SHIRIN *is worried.*

What are they going to do?

They flip their cups into the saucers.

FATEMEH *gets up and starts writing down an inventory of what they have.*

SHIRIN *is googling for more information.*

FATEMEH *makes a list of meals.*

FATEMEH *takes her sister's cup and reads the grains.*

The circle is complete at the bottom of the cup. This means you'll be at peace.

There's two women there and they're frowning.

There's a cross. Pain or illness.

There's a heart, someone is thinking about you.

There's also...what looks like...an eye.

FATEMEH *puts the cup down.*

SHIRIN *is confused by the change of energy.*

FATEMEH *gets up and goes into her room.*

She comes back out with an 'evil eye' pendant.

She hangs it on **SHIRIN***'s bedroom door.*

Mashallah. Mashallah.

SHIRIN *is touched by her sister's worry and smiles at her superstition.*

FATEMEH *grabs her book and goes into her room.*

SHIRIN *takes her sister's cup and reads the grains.*

There's commotion, lots of papers, lots of news.

The grains have gathered at the bottom. You're carrying a burden and it's still heavy.

And...

SHIRIN: A dragon?

SHIRIN *has never seen a dragon in the coffee before.*

What does it mean?

What are the qualities of a dragon?

What are the qualities of something mythical?

Something that doesn't exist?

Scene Eight

December 1978.

The radio is now playing a Christmas song.

SHIRIN *is sitting at the kitchen table. She's writing, looking very focused.*

FATEMEH *comes in from outside.*

FATEMEH: Hey.

SHIRIN: Hey.

FATEMEH: Any news?

SHIRIN: There are still demonstrations across Iran.

FATEMEH: Have you talked to Baba?

SHIRIN: Yes. Everyone is fine.

FATEMEH: That's good.

SHIRIN: Uh huh.

FATEMEH *lights a cigarette and makes coffee.* **SHIRIN** *gets up to go to her room.*

FATEMEH: Where are you going?

SHIRIN: Nowhere. Just need to write some thoughts down.

FATEMEH: Is this for your courses?

SHIRIN: Sort of. I'm thinking of writing an article for the university's newspaper.

FATEMEH: Really? What about?

SHIRIN: About what's happening in Iran.

FATEMEH: Are you serious?

SHIRIN: Yes.

FATEMEH: Is this the right time to do so?

SHIRIN: I mean, it's a revolution, it's not like it's something that happens every year.

FATEMEH: I don't think this is a good idea.

SHIRIN: Okay. Noted.

FATEMEH: It's just too risky.

SHIRIN: It's just words. In English. In Scotland.

FATEMEH: I know, but there might be consequences.

SHIRIN: The Shah is going to be overthrown.

FATEMEH: It seems that way, but you don't know for sure. And if he is overthrown, then we don't know what's going to happen next –

SHIRIN: Alright! It was just a thought. Jeez…

FATEMEH: Don't get stroppy with me.

SHIRIN: Stroppy?

FATEMEH: Yes, stroppy.

SHIRIN: I don't even know what that means.

FATEMEH: Stroppy. Stroppy…it means…annoying.

SHIRIN: You're annoying.

FATEMEH: I'm just worried.

SHIRIN: I can take care of myself.

FATEMEH: You're still a kid.

SHIRIN: So are you.

FATEMEH: Why do you always have to argue with me Shishi?

SHIRIN: I'm not, I was going to –

FATEMEH: Yes you are! Why are you so harsh with me?

SHIRIN: I…I'm sorry. I don't want to be harsh.

FATEMEH: Well you can be really…vicious. Sometimes.

SHIRIN: Sorry. I… Sorry.

FATEMEH: It's fine.

SHIRIN: …

FATEMEH: Do you want your coffee?

SHIRIN: Yeah…

They sit to drink their coffee.

FATEMEH: Did you get home fine last night?

SHIRIN: Yes.

FATEMEH: John was gone for a long time. I worried a bit.

SHIRIN: I needed food.

FATEMEH: He said.

SHIRIN: He took good care of me.

FATEMEH: He said you had a nice chat as well.

SHIRIN: Did he?

FATEMEH: He did.

They flip their cups.

SHIRIN: I barely remember it.

FATEMEH: Really?

SHIRIN: The talking was all a blur. You didn't tell me that getting drunk makes everything blurry.

FATEMEH: We're limiting you to one glass of wine next time.

You had fun though?

SHIRIN: I did. It was a good night.

FATEMEH: Great.

SHIRIN *grabs her sister's cup. She starts to read it.*

SHIRIN: I see a clear path, see here?

FATEMEH: Oh yeah? I see it.

I'm glad you and John are starting to get along.

SHIRIN: I like him. He's funnier than I thought he was.

A big clear smooth path, but at the end there's a small cross. There will be loss, but it will be small.

FATEMEH: Oh no. I don't want any more losses.

SHIRIN: There's a half moon, your inner journey is only halfway done. Still a cocoon.

You have a heart, someone is thinking of you.

FATEMEH: That's nice.

SHIRIN: There's a boat here as well. A trip maybe?

FATEMEH: A trip? I don't need a trip.

SHIRIN: Back to the motherland inshallah.

FATEMEH: Do you really want to leave that bad?

SHIRIN: For the revolution yes!

FATEMEH: I'd probably stay here.

SHIRIN: Obviously. You're in love.

FATEMEH: Even if I wasn't in love…

I wouldn't choose a life I don't want, just for him, you know that, right?

SHIRIN: I'm glad to hear that.

FATEMEH: Right.

Well dear sister, guess what I did today?

SHIRIN: What?

FATEMEH *brings out a bag full of tools.*

SHIRIN: What's all this?

FATEMEH: Our new tools.

SHIRIN: Why?

FATEMEH: To fix the window!

SHIRIN: What about the landlord?

FATEMEH: I'm not waiting for that useless toad anymore, time to take matters into our own hands.

SHIRIN: You mean into your own hands…

FATEMEH: Shishi!

The memory fades…

Scene Nine

April 2020.

The radio is playing music.

SHIRIN *is washing dishes.*

An Iranian love song from the '70s comes on.

SHIRIN *is confused.*

She tries to change the channel.

The song keeps playing.

SHIRIN *laughs.*

She enjoys the song.

A familiar voice and laughter softly filter through.

SHIRIN *listens to her own voice.*

RADIO: I wrote a poem about you. Do you want to hear it?

But you're not allowed to laugh at me!

Okay…

'Think of him.
Don't
Think of him.
Don't
Think of that escape.
The not now anymore.
You're not now anymore.
Think of just the two of you.
Nothing else.
No one else.
Where you found your loophole in time.
It's just yours.
Nothing else.
No one else.
You sway in his living room.
He sings to you in your Persian tongue.
And sparks a dream of a life you can never have.
He blows it away with his cigarette smoke
And your body is yours for the first time
In the not now
The biggest mistake of your life.
The best mistake of your life.
You felt free.
For the first time
You felt free
You felt free
You feel free.'

It's shit, isn't it?

No! Stop. You said you wouldn't laugh!

The voices fade out. She looks for her cigarettes.

She pauses. The time to quit was years ago.

She throws away the cigarettes.

Scene Ten

The radio is on.

Snippets of news.

Shah Mohammad Reza Pahlavi flees Iran.

A million march in Tehran in a show of support for the exiled Ayatollah Khomeini.

The Iranian Revolution.

The Islamic Revolution.

It's now February 1979.

FATEMEH *is on the phone their little sister, Paria.*

FATEMEH: You need to stay in school Paria.

    I know you're worried, but Baba said we should stay in Britain until things calm down.

    You know this. This was always the plan.

    You can come visit at Easter time.

    No, we're not going anywhere, both me and Shirin are staying in Scotland for now.

    I spoke to Uncle Farhad and he said that the family is fine, the foreign press is exaggerating.

At this moment, **SHIRIN** *comes home.*

FATEMEH: Okay I need to go now, Shirin's just come home.

    I will call you again soon, I promise.

    Okay, azizam.

    Bye.

SHIRIN: Salaam.

FATEMEH: Where have you been?

SHIRIN: The library.

FATEMEH: Is the library open this late?

SHIRIN: Is everything okay?

FATEMEH: Have you seen the news?

SHIRIN: Of course.

FATEMEH: Things are getting tense. Khomeini is threatening to persecute 'traitors' of the revolution.

SHIRIN: What does that mean?

FATEMEH: I don't know.

SHIRIN: We should go back.

FATEMEH: Absolutely not.

SHIRIN: Why?

FATEMEH: We still don't know what's happening –

SHIRIN: We can't have the clerics do what they want. We need leverage, we need a strong opposition, we need to organise before –

FATEMEH: You don't know what you're talking about Shirin.

SHIRIN: Stop saying that. I do. I do know what I'm talking about.

FATEMEH: We just need to wait –

SHIRIN: I'm tired of waiting! That's our city! I feel it. I feel that rage and that violence and that pain, and then I go out in the street here, and they're all oblivious. Everyone goes about their dull business while our people are literally overthrowing the government. This could be our second chance!

After we lost our first chance when the government of this country took it away from us!

FATEMEH: I understand but –

SHIRIN: No you don't understand!

FATEMEH: Listen to me –

SHIRIN: I'm done listening to you.

FATEMEH: You're being naïve!

SHIRIN: And you're being a coward!

FATEMEH: Baba says –

SHIRIN: I don't care what he's saying!

FATEMEH: Well you should.

He's the one that's actually in Iran. While you're here fantasising about being a revolutionary. He's the one dealing with actual violence. Not feelings of it.

SHIRIN: Please. He's just worried about losing his precious property.

FATEMEH: What did you just say?

SHIRIN: Nothing.

FATEMEH: What are you doing?

SHIRIN: I'm leaving.

FATEMEH: No.

SHIRIN: Yes.

FATEMEH: You're not leaving this flat.

SHIRIN: Move out of my way.

FATEMEH: Stop acting like a spoilt child!

SHIRIN: I said move out of my way.

FATEMEH: No. You're not leaving.

SHIRIN: I'm not asking for permission

FATEMEH: You're not going anywhere.

FATEMEH *attempts to physically block* **SHIRIN**.

SHIRIN: GET OUT OF MY WAY!

They struggle until **SHIRIN** *pushes* **FATEMEH** *out of the way and storms out.*

FATEMEH *is dazed and upset. She doesn't know what to do. She grabs the phone.*

FATEMEH: Hi John, it's me. I'm, Shirin…she, we had a fight and she's… she just stormed out, I don't know where she's going. I tried to stop her but she pushed me. I don't…I don't know, I just, I don't know.

Okay… Okay, oh thank you. Yes, that would be amazing. Alright, I'll start phoning everyone she knows. I'll do that. Okay. I will.

The memory fades…

Scene Eleven

April 2020.

SHIRIN *is working on a jigsaw puzzle.*

FATEMEH *is baking. She's been baking loads lately.*

SHIRIN *puts on the radio. The news comes on.*

Cases soar all over the world.

Boris Johnson has been released from hospital.

Anti-government protests erupt in Iran after Ukraine Flight 752 was shot down.

SHIRIN *switches the station to music.*

She starts to do her stretches.

FATEMEH *turns up the volume on the radio.*

She joins her sister in the stretches.

The sisters are doing different sets of stretches but are in sync.

It doesn't feel awkward.

It feels harmonious.

SHIRIN *remembers when they used to dance together to Boney M. (or was it ABBA?) in this room.*

FATEMEH *remembers when they used to dance together to Googoosh in this room.*

FATEMEH's *phone rings.*

SHIRIN *lowers the volume on the radio.*

FATEMEH: Hello darling, how are you?

Yes, yes we saw that.

We're alright, we're getting on just fine. We miss you all, that's the only thing. How are the kids?

Oh poor things, it's so difficult to explain when we don't know what's happening.

They're completely incompetent. Yes. Yes, exactly.

Who knows what the true impact will be once we're all able to be together again?

Being able to touch and express affection is such an important aspect of our lives and of their formation. Must be so hard and confusing for them. Poor little ones.

Oh we're alright, just watching TV, reading, keeping ourselves busy as usual. We're doing our daily stretches, don't worry.

Thank you, thank you darling, we're alright for now, we don't need anything.

I'll look up the new rules now. Hopefully this will all be over soon.

Alright lovely, it's good to speak to you as always.

Bye darling, bye.

FATEMEH *is looking through her phone.*

She starts to write down the rules.

SHIRIN *has a snack.*

FATEMEH *finishes writing the rules and posts them on the fridge.*

SHIRIN *continues working on her jigsaw puzzle.*

Scene Twelve

March 1979.

FATEMEH *is sitting at a table. She is a mess.*

FATEMEH: Something must have happened to him.

SHIRIN: You don't know that. He disappears all the time.

FATEMEH: Not like this! What if he's hurt?

SHIRIN: Don't say that, Fatemeh.

FATEMEH: I need a smoke.

FATEMEH *smokes.*

SHIRIN: Are you sure he's missing?

FATEMEH: I haven't seen or heard from him in three weeks. Why would he disappear? Especially now? Especially now when all…this is happening.

SHIRIN: Maybe he's gone to a party? Or maybe he needed to go work in England?

FATEMEH: He's never gone so long without calling me.

SHIRIN: …

FATEMEH: I've been calling his house and nothing, I went over and no one would answer the door.

Something's wrong, I know it.

SHIRIN: Was…never mind.

FATEMEH: Was what?

SHIRIN: Was everything alright between you two?

FATEMEH: What do you mean?

SHIRIN: I mean…you don't think that maybe he just…left.

FATEMEH: What?

SHIRIN: I'm not saying he did. I'm just asking because…I don't know… could he have just left?

FATEMEH: We've had fights, like all couples, I mean that's what couples do right?

SHIRIN: I guess…

FATEMEH: You don't actually think he's left me.

SHIRIN: I…I don't know, Fatemeh.

FATEMEH: I know you don't approve of him, but he's good, Shirin. He's been good to me. He told me he loved me. He said it. He told me that he wants a family, he wants children with me. We were planning –

SHIRIN: But he hasn't been good to you.

FATEMEH: What do you mean?

SHIRIN: … He disappears.

FATEMEH: Not like this though. It's usually on a weekend.

SHIRIN: He disappears on you, Fatemeh. He runs away from confrontation and then you're here obsessing –

FATEMEH: I am not obsessing!

SHIRIN: Fatemeh…

FATEMEH: What? Just say what you want to say.

SHIRIN: I don't think he cares about you in the way you care about him.

FATEMEH: Did he say something to you?

SHIRIN: …

FATEMEH: Tell me what you know.

SHIRIN: Please, Fatemeh.

Calm down and think through what you have with him, is it really love?

FATEMEH: Yes.

SHIRIN: Are you sure?

FATEMEH: Yes!

Yes, I'm sure.

SHIRIN: He doesn't love you, Fatemeh.

FATEMEH: What's happening? Why are you saying this?

SHIRIN: …

FATEMEH: Shirin?

The memory fades…

Scene Thirteen

May 2020.

Lockdown continues.

The radio is on as usual. It's playing some old pop music.

FATEMEH *is fixing the window.*

SHIRIN *is doing an arts and crafts project.*

They don't look at each other.

It doesn't feel awkward.

It feels harmonious.

Finally **SHIRIN** *holds up her artwork.*

A big shield.

It says 'Shirin's Shield.'

FATEMEH *can't quite believe* **SHIRIN** *spent all that time making it.*

SHIRIN *poses with the shield and struggles to take her own photo.*

FATEMEH *grabs a biscuit and goes to her room.*

SHIRIN *sits on her own.*

Isolation has been hard.

She begins to tidy.

The radio plays a nostalgic song.

Voices begin to filter through.

RADIO: 'Those days are gone
Those days of rapture and wonder'

I want to feel that!

Almond cake.

'Forgive her.'

Tiamat.

'Forgive her,
forgive because she is bewitched,'

Ghormeh Sabzi.

Enraged, she takes on the form of a massive sea dragon.

In today's episode!

The sea goddess, Tiamat.

Don't do that.

It's a revolution!

Rice biscuits. The one from the good bakery.

I see a tree, here.

I see prosperity.

Chicken stew.

Someone is thinking of you.

'Because your lives' fertile roots
burrow into her exiled soil and pound'

What does it feel like?

'With envy's rod her naive heart,
until it swells.'

Please.

Back to Tehran, I don't care…

Forgive her.

She brings forth the monsters of the Mesopotamia.

Forgive me.

Including the first dragons.

It's wonderful.

Whose bodies she fills with poison.

I see a knot.

Tea?

Entanglement.

Or coffee?

No familial obligation, remember?

I'm you sister!

I'm sorry.

I'm sorry.

This is scary.

I…

I'm scared.

The voices fade out.

SHIRIN *thinks about her sister.*

She wants to go knock on her door.

She can't.

She doesn't know how to talk to her sister anymore.

She doesn't know what words to use.

She doesn't know how to say them.

Scene Fourteen

March 1979.

FATEMEH *and* **SHIRIN** *are sitting at the table.*

FATEMEH: You're scaring me. What do you know?

　　Please tell me.

　　Shirin?

SHIRIN: I don't think he's disappeared.

　　And I don't think he's coming back.

　　I think he's left you.

FATEMEH: Why are you saying this?

SHIRIN: I'm so sorry.

FATEMEH: Sorry for what?

SHIRIN: I… I didn't mean… I didn't know that –

FATEMEH: What happened Shirin?

SHIRIN: Me and John…we've been…

FATEMEH: You've been what? What are you saying?

SHIRIN: We're…we've been…he said he loved me.

FATEMEH: What? I don't – I don't know – I don't understand. What are you talking about?

SHIRIN: Me and John, Fatemeh!

　　I'm talking about me and John.

　　We're…

We've been together.

We've been together more than once.

FATEMEH: What?

SHIRIN: I'm so sorry... I wanted to end it.

FATEMEH: ...

SHIRIN: He wanted to tell you, but I said no.

I wanted him to stay with you.

I couldn't bear for you to get hurt over this.

FATEMEH: You didn't want to hurt me?

SHIRIN: It wasn't supposed to mean anything!

FATEMEH: Then why did you do it? Why would you do something like this?

Why...why would you...how could you...for something that doesn't even mean anything to you?

SHIRIN: That's not... I didn't mean that... I just...

FATEMEH: Say what you mean. You seem to have a lot to say these days, so tell me exactly what you mean.

SHIRIN: I...

I'm so sorry.

FATEMEH: No. I don't give a fuck about your apologies.

SHIRIN: I didn't mean to hurt you.

FATEMEH: What did you mean? Huh? What did you mean to do then?

SHIRIN: I... I wasn't thinking.

FATEMEH: How could you do this to me?

SHIRIN: I didn't mean –

FATEMEH: Stop saying you didn't mean! I don't care what you meant to do, I care about what you've actually done.

I'm your sister!

SHIRIN: I know –

FATEMEH: YOUR SISTER!

SHIRIN: Fatemeh…

FATEMEH: DON'T YOU DARE TOUCH ME.

Don't touch me. Don't come near me. Don't even look at me.

You're disgusting, you know that?

Disgusting!

SHIRIN: …

FATEMEH: I feel sick.

SHIRIN: …

FATEMEH: So you know where he is?

SHIRIN: No.

FATEMEH: Liar.

SHIRIN: He told me he was going to tell you about us. He didn't say anything about leaving.

FATEMEH: Are you still fucking him?

SHIRIN: Fatemeh!

FATEMEH: Answer the question.

SHIRIN: …

FATEMEH: When was the last time you saw him?

SHIRIN: About a month ago.

I told him it was over, and I didn't want to see him again.

I swear.

That's what happened.

I didn't know he was going to do this.

FATEMEH: …

SHIRIN: I thought – I thought he was going to end things with you.

I thought he was going to tell you.

FATEMEH: Tell me about you?

SHIRIN: No… I don't know. I thought he was going to leave, but not like this.

FATEMEH: …

SHIRIN: I didn't want to hurt you.

FATEMEH: …

SHIRIN: I'm a terrible person.

FATEMEH: …

SHIRIN: I'm so sorry I did this.

FATEMEH: …

SHIRIN: I ended it. I swear… I didn't want this to happen.

FATEMEH: You need to get out.

SHIRIN: Fatemeh, please…

FATEMEH: Get out now.

SHIRIN: And go where?

FATEMEH: I don't care, you need to leave here now.

SHIRIN: But… I don't –

FATEMEH: Go stay with your beloved John.

SHIRIN: Fatemeh, that's not –

FATEMEH: Get out now!

SHIRIN: You're just gonna throw me out on the streets?

FATEMEH: Get the fuck out of my house.

Miss fucking feminist.

SHIRIN: Please…

FATEMEH: You're not welcome here anymore.

You need to leave now.

I don't want to see your face again.

Get out.

SHIRIN: What about my stuff?

FATEMEH: I'll make sure you get it.

Out!

SHIRIN *leaves reluctantly.*

FATEMEH *slams the door behind her and begins to pace as the painful realisation hits her in waves.*

She begins to punch pillows and scream into them.

She wants to cry but it hurts too much.

The shock is too much.

She gets up and blasts the radio.

She really wants to smash things but can't.

She gets an idea.

She goes into **SHIRIN**'s *room and comes out carrying piles of* **SHIRIN**'s *stuff.*

She opens the windows.

She hesitates.

Fuck it.

She throws all of it out.

She goes back to the room and grabs more stuff and throws that out as well.

The neighbours below start banging on the ceiling.

FATEMEH *bangs back, shouting FUCK YOU!*

She puts the radio up even louder.

She grabs her coat and goes out, slamming the door behind her.

The memory fades…

Scene Fifteen

May 2020.

The sisters are reading each other's coffee cups.

The circle of happiness is incomplete.

I see an open path for you. You will walk it with ease.

I see loss.

I see a small heart. Someone cares for you.

You will receive some news next to the number three.

I see a small girl with her arms reaching out.

I see lightness. You will shed your worries.

I see a knot. Entanglement.

I see a boat. You might take a journey somewhere far away.

I see light. Lots of light. This is joy.

I see a cross. Pain is present here.

I see a man with luscious hair.

I see a tower.

I see you standing there.

I see you wearing a big headdress. What's that supposed to mean? A celebration maybe.

I see the moon. A shift. A cycle will come to an end.

I see jealousy. Destructive jealousy. Someone has their eye on your happiness.

I see peace and calm.

There's a fish. Money coming in or going out.

There's a ring. A union of some sort?

There's a snake. A threat?

There's a big cloud or fog at the top of the cup.

I see a star. Luck is on your side.

SHIRIN *stretches.*

FATEMEH *bakes.*

The radio is on.

SHIRIN *does her jigsaw.*

FATEMEH *dances.*

The sound of laughter.

The crisp air of spring.

The sound of prayers and blessings.

She never learned how to sing.

She never learned to play an instrument.

She never learned to make proper tea, like a true Iranian.

She misses the textures, the colours, the sounds.

A cup of coffee and a cigarette.

SHIRIN *reads.*

FATEMEH *watches TV.*

She makes a list.

They have tea.

They drink coffee.

They remember.

SHIRIN *stretches.*

FATEMEH *speaks on the phone.*

They read coffee grounds.

I see a small heart. Someone cares about you.

Full moon. Your inner journey will come to a full circle.

Scene Sixteen

March 1979.

FATEMEH *is making a grocery list. There's a knock on the door.*

FATEMEH *opens the door,* **SHIRIN** *walks in.*

SHIRIN: Salaam.

FATEMEH: I thought I said I don't want to see you.

SHIRIN: I know.

FATEMEH: Goodbye then.

SHIRIN: Fatemeh, wait. Please.

FATEMEH: What do you want?

SHIRIN: I need to talk to you.

FATEMEH: I don't care. I don't want to talk to you.

SHIRIN: Please, Fatemeh. Please can I come in?

FATEMEH: No.

SHIRIN: Fatemeh I know I hurt you but I'm your sister!

FATEMEH: You don't get to do that.

I don't have to have you in my life just because you're my sister.

I say no to familial obligation.

Just like you.

SHIRIN: Fatemeh please…

FATEMEH: I can't trust you. You need to leave now.

SHIRIN: I'm pregnant!

FATEMEH: …

SHIRIN: I don't know what to do. I swear I wouldn't be here if I had anywhere else to go.

FATEMEH: …

FATEMEH *lets* **SHIRIN** *into the flat. She gestures at her to sit down.*

SHIRIN: I know I don't deserve it, but I need your help.

FATEMEH: Is it his?

SHIRIN: Yes.

FATEMEH: Does he know?

SHIRIN: I… I don't know where he is. I haven't been able to find him.

FATEMEH: How far along are you?

SHIRIN: About seven weeks? I'm… I'm not sure.

FATEMEH: What do you want to do?

SHIRIN: What?

FATEMEH: Do you want to keep the baby?

SHIRIN: …no.

FATEMEH: …

Baba is selling the house in Iran.

He's using the money to buy this flat.

SHIRIN: Fatemeh?

FATEMEH: …

SHIRIN: I'm scared.

FATEMEH: This is deeply unfair.

SHIRIN: I'm sorry.

FATEMEH: Enough. Stop saying sorry, I don't care if you are.

SHIRIN: I know.

FATEMEH: Be quiet.

SHIRIN: Okay…

FATEMEH: I'm done listening to you. I don't want to hear another word from you.

SHIRIN: *(nods)*

FATEMEH: …

>I will help you get a termination.

>You can stay here while you recover.

>And then I want you to leave. This time for good.

>Sleep on the streets, go back to Tehran, I don't care, as long as it's not here.

>Understood?

SHIRIN: Understood.

>Thank you.

FATEMEH: I'm not doing this for you.

Time begins to move forward.

SHIRIN *has the termination.*

FATEMEH *cares for her.*

SHIRIN *waits to be kicked out, but it never happens.*

The radio flickers on. It plays music. Voices seep out.

RADIO: I'm sorry.

>Please just say something.

>Do you want a coffee? Fatemeh?

>FATEMEH!

SHIRIN *tidies.*

FATEMEH *watches TV.*

News snippets.

Siege at Iranian Embassy in London ends as the SAS and police storm the building.

John Lennon is assassinated.

The Royal Wedding at St. Paul's Cathedral.

Iraq invades Iran.

RADIO: So how was your day? Mine was good, thanks. The kids were genuinely awful today, I think I might quit, what do you think? You can provide for the both of us. I think that's a great plan!

FATEMEH *is asleep in the armchair.*

SHIRIN *leaves biscuits in the broken cupboard.*

News snippets.

Spielberg's ET is released.

The Chernobyl Disaster.

The First Intifada breaks out.

The wreckage of the Titanic is discovered off the coast of Newfoundland.

RADIO: Did you talk to Paria today? Yes? No? I hate this, you know. I know you don't care, and you're right but I hate this. It's cruel. You're just being cruel right now.

FATEMEH *gets up to make coffee. She notices the broken cupboard. She finds the biscuits.*

SHIRIN *writes poetry.*

News snippets.

Tiananmen Square protests.

The Fall of the Berlin Wall.

Nelson Mandela is elected as President of South Africa. It's the end of Apartheid.

RADIO: Please just say something. Anything.

    Please. I can't do this anymore.

White noise.

FATEMEH *makes tea.*

SHIRIN *puts on a favourite song.*

They both softly dance along.

They don't look at each other.

They form a life together.

It feels harmonious.

Scene Seventeen

May 2020.

The radio is on.

FATEMEH *is reading.*

She gets up to start her stretches.

SHIRIN *is not up yet.*

It's late. She should be up by now.

She knocks on the door.

She makes coffee.

She sings along with the radio.

No sign of **SHIRIN**.

She turns the radio off.

She knocks on the door again.

FATEMEH: Shirin?

No answer.

FATEMEH *has a bad feeling overcome her.*

She knocks one last time.

FATEMEH: Shirin, the coffee's ready.

FATEMEH *finally has the courage to go in.*

She stays there for a while.

When she walks back out, she seems calm.

She picks up her phone and calls her niece.

FATEMEH: Hi Maryam. I'm sorry to call you like this…

It's your aunt, she's…

I don't know, she's not moving, she's not breathing.

No I haven't called an ambulance, I think… I think she's gone. I don't know…

Can you…? Yes, yes I'm so sorry, I'm sorry to ask you darling.

I don't know how these things work. I don't know… I don't know how to this…

Thank you darling, thank you. I'll wait.

Bye.

Bye.

FATEMEH *looks around, she seems a bit lost.*

She pours out two cups of coffee and puts them in the usual spot.

She drinks the coffee.

SHIRIN, *the younger version of herself, walks out of the room.*

She sits down and drinks her coffee.

FATEMEH *watches her finishing her coffee.*

They both finish drinking, they flip their cups and wait for the grounds to dry.

They pick up one another's cups and start reading.

SHIRIN: I see a giant wave.

    You'll come up against a big challenge but you have the tools to overcome it.

    I see a man with long hair. Maybe you'll finally meet the love of your life.

FATEMEH: I see wings, like a butterfly.

    You've completed a cycle.

SHIRIN: I see a big heart. Someone cares for you and is thinking about you.

    I see commotion. You will maybe have a party with lots of food.

FATEMEH: I see a woman, she might be close to you. She's got her eye on you.

    Be careful.

SHIRIN: There's a clear, open path, you will eventually overcome all obstacles.

FATEMEH: I don't know what to do.

SHIRIN: About what?

FATEMEH: I couldn't even call an ambulance.

SHIRIN: It's okay.

    We get to have one last coffee together.

FATEMEH: I don't want to drink coffee alone.

SHIRIN: Then don't.

FATEMEH: …

SHIRIN: …

FATEMEH: I always thought I would go before you.

SHIRIN: Because you're older?

FATEMEH: Our family did it all wrong.

We died all wrong.

FATEMEH: Do you think it's too late to start over?

SHIRIN: It's never too late to start over.

FATEMEH: Maybe it's time to go back to Tehran.

SHIRIN: Do you miss it?

FATEMEH: I do.

I'm scared to go back.

SHIRIN: Why?

FATEMEH: What if it's not the Tehran that we left?

I mean, what a question, of course it's not the same place.

SHIRIN: One way to find out.

FATEMEH: I don't want to go alone.

SHIRIN: Then let's go together.

FATEMEH: Yes.

I'm sorry.

I'm sorry for everything.

SHIRIN: I know.

And I forgive you.

I always have.

You knew that, right?

The radio switches on and tunes in.

The sound of children's voices.

RADIO: HELLO AND WELCOME TO OUR SHOW! THIS IS…
SISTER RADIO!

I would like to welcome today our very special guest, my real actual
sister… Shirin! Shirin, can you tell us what your favourite game is?

My favourite is…it's… I like to play 'RADIO' with my big sister
Fatemeh. Sometimes our sister Paria joins as well, but she's a baby so
she can't talk yet.

And why is it your favourite game?

I like it because…we get to play it together.

SHIRIN *holds her sister's hand.*

They listen in silence.

They try to remember who they were in Tehran.

End.